HIBERNIAN
18 75
EDINBURGH

THE OFFICIAL
HIBERNIAN
FOOTBALL CLUB ANNUAL 2015

Written by David Forsyth
Designed by Cavan Convery

g

A Grange Publication

© 2014. Published by Grange Communications Ltd., Edinburgh, under licence from Hibernian Football Club. Printed in the EU.

Photographs ©SNS Group

ISBN: 978-1-910199-07-7

£7.99

CONTENTS

WELCOME TO THE OFFICIAL
HIBERNIAN
FOOTBALL CLUB
ANNUAL **2015**

Your football Club has gone through a year of significant change aimed at making Hibernian more successful on and off the pitch, more engaged with its supporters, and rooted even more firmly in the community.

To help bring about the changes we want to see, we recruited Leeann Dempster as our Chief Executive, and already we are seeing the positive difference she is making.

We have opened up the ownership of the football club, creating more shareholders and ensuring our supporters have a meaningful voice in our decision taking, with supporters now able to directly influence who represents them in the Boardroom.

We have brought a dynamic and modern Head Coach to the Club, backed by a progressive backroom team, to ensure we provide our players with the best possible platform to bring us the sporting success we all want.

Through the Hibernian Community Foundation, we are touching more lives and making an even greater difference to people in our community through encouraging more active living, through learning opportunities, through helping people find work and many other ways.

Of course, during the past year, we have suffered the crushing disappointment of relegation, but now we are rebuilding to create a club that everyone who cares about Hibernian will be proud of.

Meantime, I hope you enjoy the Annual.

Rod Petrie

LEEANN TAKES OVER AS CHIEF EXECUTIVE

Chairman Rod Petrie made a shrewd signing in the summer when he successfully head-hunted LEEANN DEMPSTER to take on the role as Chief Executive at Hibernian.

Leeann joined after a very successful spell at Motherwell FC, attracted by the huge potential she saw in Hibernian, its big support, and its infrastructure.

While she has a reputation for strong supporter and community engagement, Leeann understands that delivering a successful football club is key to progress. She appointed George Craig Head of Football Operations to help her oversee and overhaul, and then they sought out a new man to manage the Club's on field advancement, Alan Stubbs.

Leeann's vision for the Club is ambitious, but she insists it is achievable with everyone working together: "I want the Club to be successful on and off the pitch. That means a team that plays winning and attractive football, and it means a Club rooted in its community and engaged fully with its supporters.

"The Club has to become a real hub and a genuine asset in the community, and something that every Hibernian supporter can be proud of."

HEAD COACH
AT THE HELM

ALAN STUBBS' arrival as Head Coach of Hibernian, marked the start of a new sense of optimism at the Club.

Bringing with him an experienced backroom team in John Doolan and Andy Holden – both, like himself, having strong links to Liverpool – he has set about rebuilding the Club's onfield fortunes.

The Hibernian job may be his first at the helm of a Club, but his experience managing the reserve team at Everton, where he had a bigger staff and player pool than at Easter Road, has stood him in good stead.

And he has been able to rely on the advice and assistance of his two coaches,

John Doolan – who left a job as first team coach at Wigan to come north, and Andy Holden – who worked with Alan in the Davie Moyes era at Everton.

Alan said: "I've known both John and Andy for a long time, and they are both fantastic coaches and fantastic men. We all share the same ideas and values, and that is a real support to me."

continued...

HEAD COACH
AT THE HELM
...continued

A former centre back, Alan enjoyed a long and successful playing career. In England, his clubs included Bolton Wanderers, Sunderland and Derby County, but he is of course, most closely associated with the team he grew up supporting and where he enjoyed two spells as a player – Everton.

However in Scotland, he is best remembered for a five-year spell spent at the heart of defence in a hugely entertaining Celtic side – a period in which he memorably made his comeback from fighting a serious illness at Easter

Road, to warm applause from both Celtic and Hibernian fans.

Alan is determined to be seen as his own man, with his own style, but acknowledges

the influences of the excellent managers he worked with during his career as player and coach, including Bruce Rioch, Davie Moyes, and Roberto Martinez.

Of his philosophy, he is simple and straightforward: "I want to win games – it is about winning first and foremost. But I also want to play good, passing football that will entertain the fans. So that's it, winning, and playing good football to win."

At the time of his appointment, Alan said: "To be given this opportunity with Hibernian is a great privilege and a real honour, it is a massive club with huge potential.

"I'm excited about the future here at Hibernian and what we can all achieve together at the club – this is the start of the journey.

"The Scottish Championship will be a tough division, but I'm confident that if we approach the challenge with enthusiasm, optimism and belief then we can achieve success."

Alan was the first appointment made by the Club's new Chief Executive, Leeann Dempster, who joined in the summer after a successful spell at Motherwell. She said: "It's important that the CEO and Head Coach are very much on the same page and that they forge a close working and trusting partnership.

I spoke with Alan and it became apparent early in the discussions that we had a common goal.

"He is a driven, intelligent and strong-minded character, who has a very clear vision about what he wants to achieve in football – producing positive results, playing attractive football and developing young players.

"All those attributes fitted the criteria we required and we're

confident Alan is the right man to unite the club and bring success to Hibernian."

FIND SUNSHINE'S FLAG

Sunshine has only gone and left his Hibernian flag behind!

Trouble is, he can't remember which entrance leads him to it?

Can you help him find the right way?

Answers on page 58

13

KID'S KIT
COMPETITION

FANCY SCORING A COMPLETE HIBERNIAN KID'S KIT?

You could find yourself kitted out head to toe with the fantastic 2014/15 strip, shorts and socks.

Not only that, but the strip will be autographed! There's only one way to find out who by, and that's to enter!

We would like to know why you love being a Hibee in no more than 50 words.

Answer to start with:
"I love being a Hibee because…"

TO ENTER:

You can enter one of two ways:

By Email: Please submit your email entry to frontdesk@grangecommunications.co.uk with KID'S KIT COMPETITION in the subject line.

By Post: Please submit your entry on a postcard addressed to –

2015 Hibernian FC Kid's Kit Competition,
Grange Communications Ltd,
22 Great King Street,
Edinburgh,
EH3 6QH.

Please note: Entrants must provide their full name, current address, and a daytime telephone number in order to make a valid entry.

TERMS AND CONDITIONS
2015 Hibernian FC Competition
Entry

1. Grange Communications Ltd (whose registered office is 22 Great King Street, Edinburgh, EH3 6QH) is the promoter of the 2015 Hibernian FC Annual Kid's Kit Competition Prize Draw (the "**Prize Draw**").

2. By entering the Prize Draw entrants agree to be bound by these terms and conditions ("**Conditions**") and confirm that all information submitted is true, accurate and complete. Grange Communications Ltd reserves the right to verify the eligibility of any and all entrants and may, in its sole discretion, disqualify any entrant that fails to satisfy the eligibility requirements. Entrants shall at all times act in good faith towards Grange Communications Ltd and the Prize Draw.

3. Employees of Grange Communications Ltd or Hibernian FC or any of their associated companies or subsidiaries (and their families) are excluded from entering the Prize Draw.

4. Entry into the Prize Draw is free (except for any standard cost of postage) and on the basis of one entry per person.

5. In order to enter the Prize Draw and to be considered for the Prize, entrants must submit their entries to
Grange Communications Ltd either by email to frontdesk@grangecommunications.co.uk with KID'S KIT COMPETITION in the subject line or by postcard addressed to 2015 Hibernian FC Kid's Kit Competition, Grange Communications Ltd, 22 Great King Street, Edinburgh, EH3 6QH. Entrants must provide their full name, current address and a daytime telephone number in order to make a valid entry.

6. The Prize Draw will close at 12:00 GMT on Friday 27th March 2015 (the "**Closing Date**") and any entries received after the Closing Date will not be entered into the Prize Draw. The Prize Draw will take place as soon as reasonably practicable following the Closing Date.

Prize

7. Subject to paragraph 8, the prize will consist of one Hibernian FC Kid's Kit for Season 2014/15 (the "**Prize**"). The winner (the "**Winner**") of the Prize will be given a choice of size and of kit when they are informed of their win.

8. Grange Communications Ltd reserves the right to substitute the Prize with another of a similar nature at any time.

9. The Prize is non-transferable and there is no cash alternative.

Winner

10. The winner will be selected at random from all valid entries received on or before the Closing Date.

11. Only the Winner of the Prize Draw will receive notification from Grange Communications Ltd. The Winner will be notified by email or telephone as soon as practicable after the Closing Date. Following the draw, the Prize will be posted to the Winner at the address submitted in the Winner's entry.

15

NEW RECRUITS

FARID EL ALAGUI

The capture of French-Moroccan player Farid El Alagui saw the Club gain the experienced striker it needed to increase competition and goals up front.

At 6ft 1in and weighing in at more than 13 stones, the powerful El Alagui offers a number of strengths — he is strong and quick with an excellent touch.

Farid has already had a positive spell in the Scottish Championship with Falkirk when he finished up top scorer.

DAVID GRAY

David Gray was Alan Stubbs first signing, the right back joined in the summer on a two-year contract.

David started his professional career across the city at Hearts, moving at a young age to join Manchester United where he spent several years. He also had spells at a number of other English clubs.

Quick to overlap and strong in defence, David delighted Hibernian fans with a goal on his debut in a pre-season friendly at Berwick.

NEW RECRUITS

CALLUM BOOTH

Whilst Academy graduate Callum has always been a Hibernian player, after having spent the best part of two seasons on loan, his return to Easter Road felt like welcoming a new arrival.

The left back continued his development during his loan spells at Livingston and Raith Rovers, and his recall to Hibernian means he can continue to excite supporters at Easter Road with his bold attacking allied – to more streetwise defending learned in his Championship spells.

ALAN COMBE

Hibernian fan Alan Combe finally joined the Club as a player coach. The man who has served as goalkeeper for a host of Scottish clubs, most notably Dundee United and Kilmarnock, is now the man Hibernian largely depends on for keeping out the opposition.

Alan is not only responsible for coaching our number one keeper, at the age of 40 he remains superbly fit and is registered as a player, also acting as goalie back-up.

Leith born and bred, Alan's great-uncle was Bobby Combe, one of the stars of the 'Famous Five' era.

CROSSWORD PUZZLE

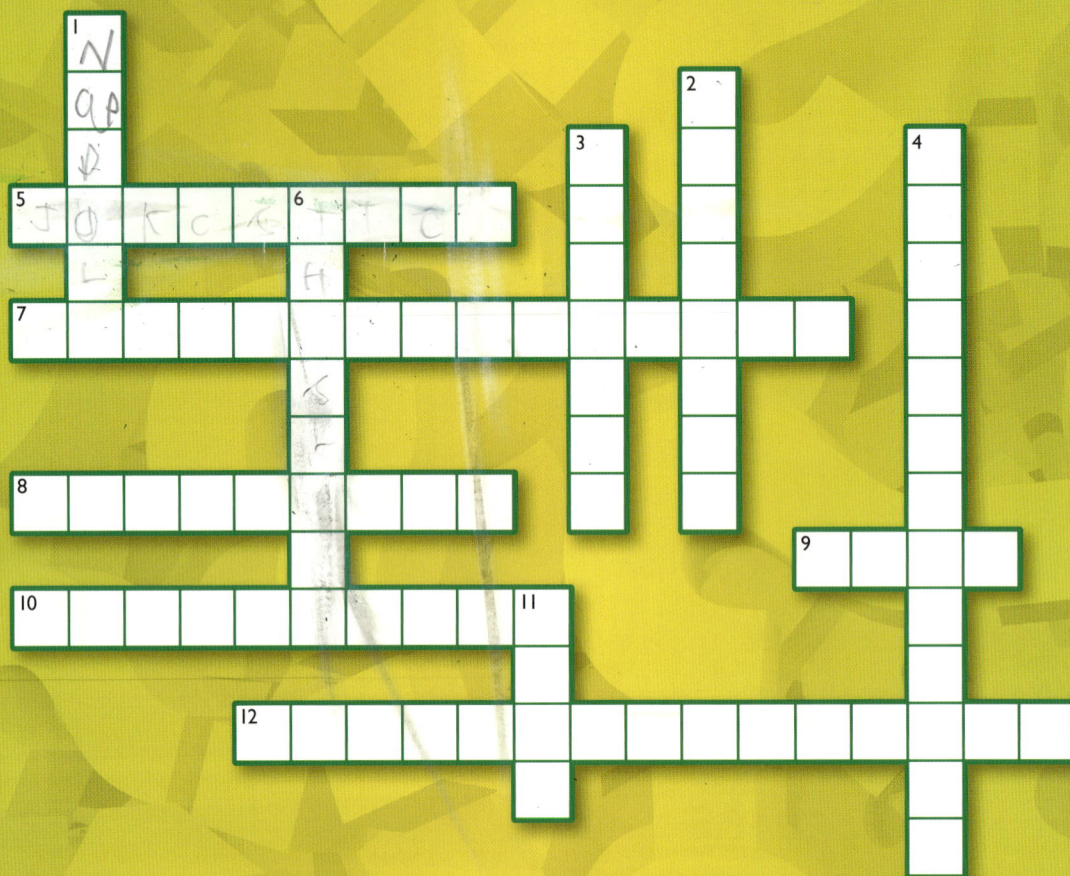

DOWN

1 Which Italian club did Hibs defeat 5-0 at Easter Road in the Fairs Cup in 1967? (6)

2 What does the name 'Hibernian' mean? (8)

3 Where did Hibernian go on a pre-season tour in July 2005? (7)

4 Which former Hibernian star was selected for Trinidad & Tobago during the 2006 World Cup finals? (7,6)

6 What famous Easter Road characteristic disappeared in season 1999/2000? (3,5)

11 Name the aquatic singer who backs the Hibees. (4)

ACROSS

5 Who was the Manager when Hibernian played a friendly against Real Madrid in 1964? (4,5)

7 Name the first Captain of Hibernian. (7,8)

8 Goalkeeper Inducted to the Hibernian Hall of Fame. (4,5)

9 Name the Scottish singer who sang at Easter Road stadium in 2005. (4)

10 Which position does Jordan Forster play? (6,4)

12 What is the North Stand at Easter Road called? (6,4,5)

Answers on page 58

20

FAMOUS FACES

The six faces below are all Hibees fans, but can you guess who each one is?

1 TV Presenter

2 Comedian

3 Musician

4 Actor

5 Sportsperson

6 Author

Answers on page 59

RUSSELL LATAPY

Known as the 'Little Magician' – the maestro from Trinidad and Tobago, whose brand of sparkling football would bring him a warm place in the hearts of Hibernian supporters.

Russell Latapy was a virtual unknown in Scotland when he signed for Hibernian in October 1998, even though when he was brought to the Club by then Manager – Alex McLeish, he had performed in championship winning sides in Portugal, notably Boavista and Porto, playing under none other than manager, Sir Bobby Robson.

But it wasn't long before his name was being sung and chanted at Easter Road with huge affection and reverence, as a number of stunning and match-winning performances cemented his reputation as one of the Club's all-time great entertainers.

Friend and Trinidad and Tobago team-mate Tony Rougier had recommended Latapy to McLeish, who invited the then 30 year-old to participate in a bounce match against Brechin. It took just a few minutes for the little man's eye-catching talent to make up the manager's mind.

The Club was playing in the First Division and during the season Latapy lived up to his nickname – 'Little Magician', as he played a pivotal role when the team ran away with the

He was also instrumental in helping bring about a memorable pre-season tour to Trinidad & Tobago, where Hibernian supporters were able to witness for themselves the enormous respect for Russell in his homeland.

A colossally important player, Latapy then ascended to the loftiest pinnacle of any Hibernian folk-hero, when he helped to break Hearts in the famous 6-2 derby demolition at Easter Road on 22 October, 2000.

Hearts manager Jim Jeffries and his team, later ruefully confirmed that they were powerless to prevent Latapy from annihilating the team in maroon, as he was the person who all eyes were on, despite Hibernian containing a host of luminaries that day, including hat-trick hero – Mixu Paatelainen.

championship. He was duly voted – First Division Player of the Year at the end of his most productive season, in terms of his goals-to-games ratio, this came during the following campaign when he scored 12 goals to help Hibernian consolidate their place in the Scottish Premier League.

Russell's departure after two-and-a-half sparkling years, was to be an abrupt one. His atrocious time-keeping and love of a night out on the town (with close friend Dwight Yorke), proved a lapse of discipline too far.

Nonetheless, Russell's reign at Easter Road ensured the little man from the Caribbean, truly did bring Sunshine on Leith.

HEALTHY HIBEES

the Hibernian Community Foundation

TOUGH MUDDER

2014 has be a seminal year for our health programmes, delivering three 'Fit Fans in Training' courses, four 'Healthy Hibees' programmes and our all-year round 'Fit for Change' sessions. It has been a year for many Hibees to take control of their health, by visiting Easter Road and joining one of the courses that help them live a more active life.

Fit Fans in Training is a government funded 12-week programme, assisting men aged 35 – 65 years old to lose weight and get fit. To register for 'FFIT', take some measurements: belly – at least 40 inches or trouser waist of 38 inches, and a BMI of 25+.

The Healthy Hibees courses are suitable for people of all ages who are interested in increasing fitness, managing weight and achieving personal goals. Throughout the courses, participants will gain access to health promotion information and basic health screening. The 12-week courses are based in the South Stand at Easter Road Stadium, and Hibernian Training Centre offer a wide range

of activities including yoga, walking, diet and nutrition guidance, and fitness challenges.

Fit for Change is an all year round programme promoting health, fitness and wellbeing for men and women, organised around the principles of setting personal goals, being active and making healthy choices.

Many have taken part in challenges that would not have been possible before getting involved in one of our health programmes. Such as Tough Mudder – over 12 miles in mud with obstacles from ice, electric cables and wall climbs, all achieved by men who previously would have had difficulty even running for a bus!

In May, 48 graduates exceeded all expectations by running 1,368 laps of the hallowed Easter Road turf, which equates to over 13 full marathons.

Overall, since these fitness programmes began, Hibs' fans have lost an incredible 840kg, which is roughly the same weight as the entire first team! Adding up the inches lost from their waists, the would stretch from the goal line to the edge of the penalty box.

It's been an exciting 2014, and 2015 will be even more exciting with Hibernian's involvement in the community.

Health is part of Hibernian, and we aim to increase activity and reach many more with the opportunity of living a healthier and longer life.

For more information on the work of the foundation visit:
www.hibernianinthecommunity.org.uk

HIBERNIAN COMMUNITY FOUNDATION

learning, health & opportunity

SCOTTISH CHARITY NO: SC039699

PLAYER PORTRAITS

PAUL HANLON came through the ranks of the Hibernian Academy, making an early breakthrough into the first team following a productive loan spell at St Johnstone, and has become established in the squad ever since.

The cultured defender has captained Scotland at under 21 level, as well as captaining Hibernian. Paul missed the end of last season through injury, when his presence and ability was sorely missed.

HIBERNIAN

18 75

EDINBURGH

LEWIS STEVENSON is the Club's longest-serving player, and a model of consistency. Whether played at full back or in midfield, he never gives less than his best.

A dedicated professional, astonishingly Lewis made his debut almost ten years ago, in 2005. He played a major role in the unforgettable 5-1 League Cup win over Kilmarnock, earning the Man of the Match award in the process.

LIAM CRAIG is an accomplished midfielder who joined Hibernian after several successful seasons with St Johnstone.

He was named Captain in his debut season 2013-14, and also achieved the distinction of scoring the winning goal in a New Year derby at Easter Road. Liam will be hoping to lead the team to greater success going forward.

ALEX HARRIS is another graduate of the Hibernian Academy who broke into the first team under Pat Fenlon's management in season 2012-13, and quickly established himself as a talent to watch.

The attacking midfielder enjoyed several Man of the Match performances, and played a huge part in turning around a 0-3 half-time deficit in the Scottish Cup semi final against Falkirk, which was eventually won 4-3.

JORDON FORSTER is another young defender with huge potential. Big, strong, aggressive and confident, he has many of the qualities needed to make it at the top level. Which he showed making a confident debut centre-half at Tynecastle.

While his main role is in stopping opposition attacks and goals, Jordon has shown that he can be a real threat in the opposition box from set-pieces.

SAM STANTON is a talented midfielder who also came through the ranks at Hibernian, making his first team debut against Rangers in January 2012 as a substitute.

However it wasn't until last season that he established himself as a regular-starter. His close control, willingness to take on defenders, and his ability from free kicks, have made him a fans favourite.

SCOTT ROBERTSON joined the club from Blackpool in January 2013. His experience, after spells in England and most notably, with Dundee United, made him an important recruitment but injury hindered his first season at Hibernian.

Capped twice by Scotland, his experience and his box-to-box style, will be vital for Hibernian in the quest to return to Scottish football's top flight.

DANNY HANDLING made his debut in May 2011, coming on as a substitute in a match against Aberdeen. A youth team-mate of Alex Harris at Civil Service Strollers, he's an attacking player who can play in behind the strikers.

Danny has been capped at several youth levels for Scotland, including: under 17, under 20 (when he captained the team), and was selected for the squad at under 21 level last year before being forced to withdraw through injury.

PAUL HEFFERNAN will be a key man in ensuring Hibernian score the goals they will need to gain promotion from the Championship.

The experienced striker has a proven track record within Scottish football in the top flight, after joining Hibernian in the summer of 2013, after a successful spell at Kilmarnock. His first season at Hibernian was blighted by injury, he will be hoping to enjoy a better level of fitness for the 2014/15 season.

JASON CUMMINGS is a left-sided striker who joined Hibernian in 2013 from Hutcheson Vale. He made his first team debut in a match against Inverness, after showing great goal-scoring form for the under 20s side.

Confident in his own ability, Jason played through a lean spell before hitting scoring form towards the end of 2013/14 season. He hopes to build on that early success throughout the course of the year.

FUR IT'S A GRAND OLD
TEAM TO PLAY FUR

JOIN
HIBS
KIDS

The coolest cat in the world, Sunshine the
Leith Lynx wants to offer all of his wee pals
the purr-fect deal – become a Hibs Kids
Member and get ready to roar the Hibees
on to victory this season.

When you sign up to become a member of
Hibs Kids you will now be entitled to a ticket
for the following post Christmas games:

Hibernian v Livingston, March 2015
Hibernian v Queen of the South April 2015

Guess what? The price of Hibs Kids
Membership has been frozen again this
season, so it's only £10.

Remember as a Hibs Kid Season Ticket
Member you are also entitled to "Bring a
Friend" at the FIVE games for £10 Adults
and £5 Concessions.

Find out about all the membership benefits
and join at hibernianfc.co.uk or call
0844 844 1875 option 2

ALEX
HARRIS

WHO AM I?

Can you guess who these past Hibernian players are based on the facts given below? Go on, give it your best shot!

1

Joined Hibernian in 1999

Lost his front teeth during a game

English was not his first language

ANSWER _ _ _ _ _ _   _ _ _ _ _ _ 6, 6

2

Scottish Parents but born in Liverpool

Started playing for Hibernian at age 17

Elder brother also played for the club

ANSWER _ _ _   _ _ _ _ _ 3, 5

3

Born in 1928

A member of the 'Famous Five'

Most capped Hibernian player

ANSWER _ _ _ _ _ _ _   _ _ _ _ _ _ 6, 6

4

Edinburgh Born

Made over 700 appearances

Scored 364 goals

ANSWER _ _ _ _ _ _   _ _ _ _ _ 6, 5

Answers on page 59

5

Hibernian player for 13 years

Captained the team when they won the Scottish League Cup Final in 1972

As well as captain, he also became Manager of the Club

ANSWER _ _ _ _ _ _ _ _ _ _ 3, 7

6

Born in Falkirk

Holds the record for most League appearances

Scored twice in the 7-0 victory against Hearts in 1973

ANSWER _ _ _ _ _ _ _ _ _ _ _ _ 6, 6

7

Played for Hibernian twice within his football career

Represented Scotland twice between 2002 – 2006

Versatile defender and midfielder

ANSWER _ _ _ _ _ _ _ _ _ 3, 6

8

Moved to Hibernian in 1987 for a fee of £325,000

His father had also played for Hibernian

Achieved the unusual feat for a goalkeeper by scoring a goal in a Premier Division match with a huge kick-out

ANSWER _ _ _ _ _ _ _ _ _ 4, 5

THE FAMOUS FIVE

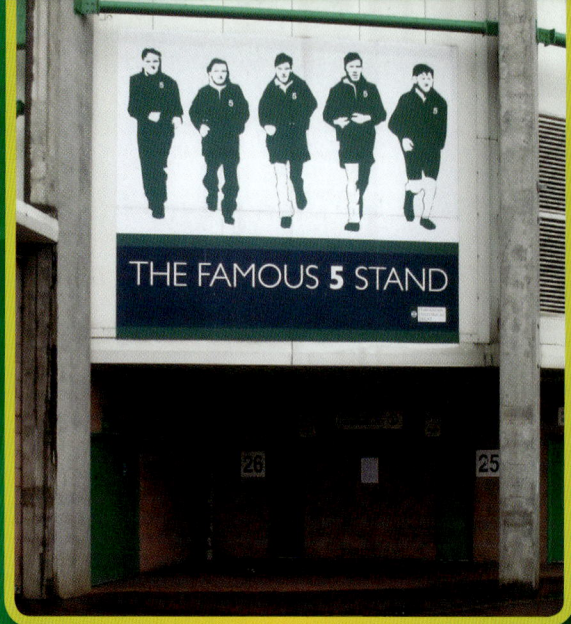

THE FAMOUS 5 STAND

The forward line that would lead the greatest Hibernian team of all time, and earn legendary status, came to be during a 2-0 victory over Queen of the South on 15 October, 1949.

For that game, a youngster from Selkirk named Bobby Johnstone joined a line-up that was soon to achieve immortality...The Famous Five.

Gordon Smith – perhaps the greatest ever player to wear the green and white of Hibernian, was the first of the five to join the club in 1941. Lawrie Reilly – the only one of the five to be born a Hibs supporter, was just 16 when he signed for the club in 1944, making his first team debut against Kilmarnock at Rugby Park the following year. Eddie Turnbull and Willie Ormond – both came from the Falkirk area, had been in the Royal Navy during the war and signed

around the same time in 1946. A few months later the irrepressible Hibs manger Willie McCartney, motored to the borders to sign the 17 year old Bobby Johnstone. No one could possibly know it then, but Johnstone would be the final cog in a machine that would in time form, arguably the greatest ever forward line produced in Scotland.

The late 1940's and early 50's was a defining period for the game. During this time

Johnstone (left) and Reilly

Lawrie (left) and Buchanan wearing a Hibs strip for first time, 1944

Hibernian, led by the Famous Five, would burst to the forefront of Scottish football, watched by crowds in unprecedented numbers. On 2 January 1950, 65,840 spectators – still the largest crowd to watch a football match in Edinburgh, crammed into Easter Road to see Hibs play their local rivals Hearts.

Between 1948 and 1953 the Easter Road club would win the league championship

The Famous Five – Smith, Johnstone, Reilly, Turnbull and Ormond

THE FAMO

three times, lose another only on goal average, and yet another by a solitary point to become the most successful side ever in the long history of the club.

At that time, while most other teams took pre-season trips to the Scottish Highlands, Hibs would regularly tour the continent, establishing a formidable reputation for themselves by competing against some of the top sides in Europe. It was this reputation that would see them invited to take part in an eight team competition in Brazil in 1953, the first Scottish side to visit the country.

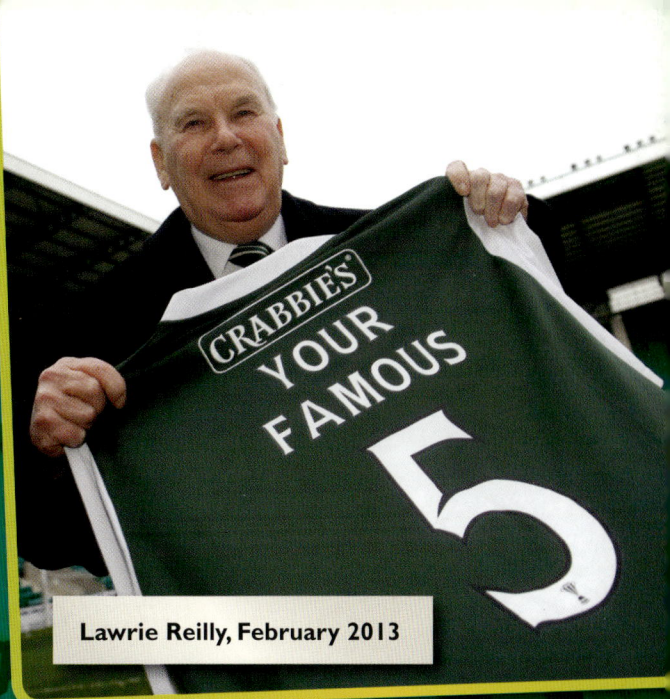

Lawrie Reilly, February 2013

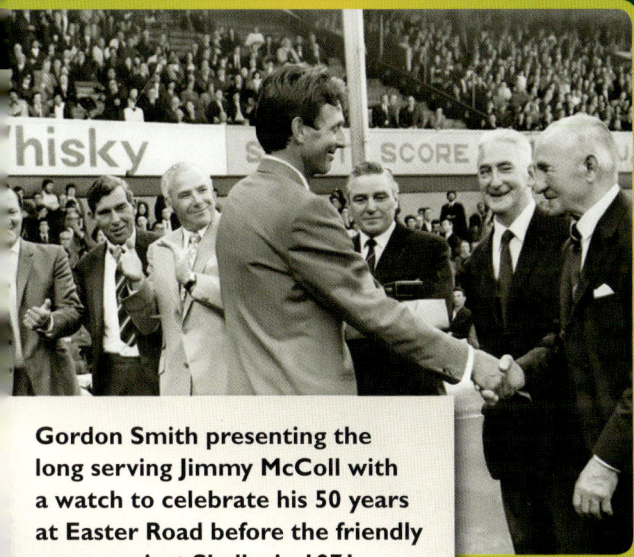

Gordon Smith presenting the long serving Jimmy McColl with a watch to celebrate his 50 years at Easter Road before the friendly game against Shalke in 1971.

In January 1955, the Famous Five played their last game as Bobby Johnstone departed to Manchester City. Perhaps surprisingly, the Famous Five had featured as a complete unit on only 109 occasions, mainly because of serious injuries received by Smith and Ormond, but during this time the magical quintet had scored 285 goals between them — a truly phenomenal record.

The remaining members of the Famous Five would all feature in the inaugural European Cup competition later that year, when Hibs became the first ever British side to take part in the new competition. Although reaching the semi-finals only to lose to French club Reims, Gordon Smith was adamant that the new tournament had arrived just a bit too late for the club. Had it come along a couple of years earlier, there was absolutely no doubt

in Smith's mind that Hibs would have won it, perhaps more than once.

In 1961, Willie Ormond, the last remaining playing member of the Famous Five, was allowed to join hometown side Falkirk, on a free transfer. Bringing to an end, a magical era for the club that is unlikely ever to be repeated.

All of the Famous Five were Scottish internationalists and all, quite rightly, have been inducted into both the Hibernian Hall of Fame at Easter Road, and that of the SFA at Hampden.

Reilly's death last year severed the last remaining links to a forward line that had enthralled football fans, not only in this country, but much further afield during what was undoubtedly a golden era for Scottish football, but the memories will linger on.

Tom Wright, Hibernian Historical Trust.

HIBERNIAN LIONHEARTS

They are the players whose wholehearted commitment and uncompromising performances, establish them as fans favourites – the lion-hearted players.

This year, we pay tribute to two great stars who have worn the green and white with distinction – Ian Murray and Erich Schaedler.

Mr Versatility – Ian Murray could play almost anywhere across defence and midfield, and was often asked to, filling in at full back, centre back and in centre and wide midfield roles.

Yet despite being moved around, he always gave 100% in every match, prompting the manager – Alex McLeish, who handed him his debut to say he: "has the heart of a lion."

Crunching in the tackle, good on the ball, and with never ending supplies of energy, Ian also served as Captain, and gained international caps at under 21 and full Scotland level.

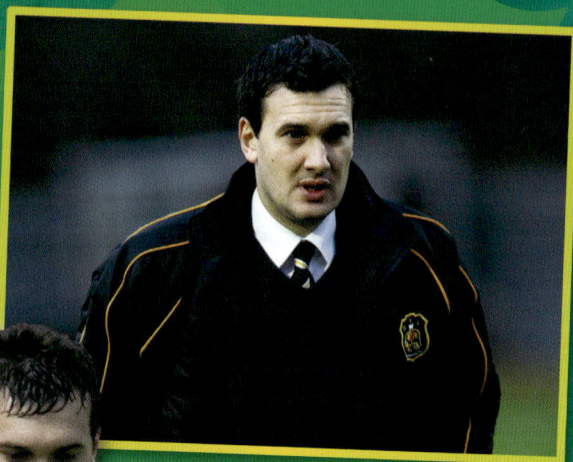

He spent two spells at the Club, 1999-2005 and 2008-2012.

After leaving the Club, he moved into coaching as player/manager at Championship side – Dumbarton.

Drybrough Cups. He also played in a certain unforgettable derby encounter at Tynecastle on New Year's Day, 1973, which ended in a famous 7-0 win.

He won one full Scotland cap when he played against West Germany in 1974, and in the same year, was a part of the World Cup squad, although he did not play in the tournament as Scotland exited on goal difference.

Erich 'Shade' Schaedler, was an important player in one of the great Hibernian sides – Turnbull's Tornadoes team of the 1970s.

The son of a German POW, Erich signed for the Club in 1969, shortly before Eddie Turnbull took over as manager. The left back was known for his strong, no-nonsense style, and for his long throws. 'Shade' was famed as a tough tackler and for his prodigious work-rate, and was a superb component in the team that enjoyed significant success in the early 1970s, winning a League Cup and two

Erich's tragic and early death at the age of 36 in 1985, was a source of great sorrow to the Hibernian community.

SPOT THE BALL

Farid El Alagui jumps to win control of the ball, but can you guess which one is the actual ball in play?

Answers on page 59

SAM
STANTON

ONE CLUB FOR LEWIS

2015 will see a remarkable milestone in the career of LEWIS STEVENSON – a decade spent in the first team at the Club he joined as a youngster.

Kirkcaldy born Lewis, is that rarest of modern phenomenon – a professional footballer, who has to date, spent his entire career at just one Club – his beloved Hibernian.

The Club's 'Mr Versatility' has chalked up well over 200 appearances in the first team, and memorably turned in a Man of the Match performance in the 5-1 League Cup Final demolition of Kilmarnock that will remain high on the list of Hibernian all-time highlights for many years to come.

Lewis was born in 1988 in Fife and attended Balwearie High School. He joined the Hibernian Academy aged just 14. He turns 27 in January 2015, meaning he has been involved with the Club for an astonishing 13 years already.

He made his competitive debut in September 2005, in a League Cup tie against Ayr United,

but didn't make his Scottish Premier League debut until the start of the following season.

From the start of his career, Lewis' big-hearted performances have endeared him to many supporters, his commitment ensuring his stature isn't simply measured in terms of his 5ft 7ins height!

Of his longevity, Stevenson said when signing his existing contract: "The Club has always been a big part of my life. If someone had told me when I joined as a 14-year-old, I would still be here all these years later I wouldn't have believed them."

Popular with his team-mates, and with all of the managers he has played under, Lewis is known for his exemplary conduct as a model professional. The Club's longest-serving player never hides and, in the words of one coach: "never sells himself short."

That attitude has seen him through his lean spells at the Club. He said: "There have been times when I've not been playing and had to prove myself. I've proved myself a few times now, and that must be a testament to me."

"BOOZY" WINGING IT

ALEX HARRIS may be nicknamed "Boozy" after former Hibernian favourite Guillaume "Boozy" Beuzelin, but it is his intoxicating brand of wing play that Hibernian fans want to see bamboozle opposing full backs.

Alex, still just 20 years old, has been associated with Hibernian since he the age of nine, and is a product of the club's Academy.

The former Edinburgh Academy pupil made his debut when he came on as a substitute against Dundee in October 2012. He made his first start against Inverness Caledonian Thistle in March 2013.

Alex burst onto the scene with a series of performances that had supporters off their seats. Pace, touch, close control and a willingness to take on opposing defenders marked him out as one of Scotland's most talked about talents.

The highlight of his career to date undoubtedly came in the Scottish Cup semi-final win over Falkirk at Hampden in the 2012/13 season, when he inspired an astonishing comeback. The team had looked down and out, trailing 3-0 at half time, before 'Boozy' hit top form, scoring a memorable goal in an eventual 4-3 victory.

He has come through the ranks with a number of team-mates, including Danny Handling and Sam Stanton. He said: "Hibs has always been renowned

for bringing through their own youngsters. It's great to see so many of us getting to be involved in the first team."

Alex hasn't enjoyed an easy ride. First he had to cope with the death of his father, Kenny, who had been a huge support to him, earlier in 2012. Sadly, his father didn't see the son he encouraged every step of the way make his debut.

Then Alex was faced with a serious ankle injury early in season 2013/14 after he had made such a big impact, and had to sit on the side-lines for the first half of the campaign.

This season, with a full pre-season behind him and a Head Coach who has high hopes for him, Alex will be looking to pick up where he so memorably left off in that stunning Cup semi-final.

Ten Facts about…
LIAM CRAIG

Joined Hibernian in summer 2013

Scored first career hat-trick in September in League Cup tie against Stranraer

Made more than 200 appearances for the Perth side

He began his professional career at Ipswich Town

Liam stands 6ft tall

Appointed Captain November 2013

Born December 27th, 1986

Joined St Johnstone, initially on loan, in 2007

A native of Chirnside, Berwickshire

Captained Ipswich youth side to victory in 2005 FA Youth Cup final

LIAM
CRAIG

ONES TO WATCH

LEWIS ALLAN

LEWIS ALLAN is a young striker with big prospects. The young Borderer has pushed his way into involvement with the first team squad this season.

Still only 17 years old, the young striker is already physically strong enough to compete at this level and his power, allied with his ability and his willingness to learn, should ensure that the future his future is bright. Despite being brought up in rugby, football runs in his blood, his father playing in the Borders alongside a certain John Collins.

He was identified by Head Coach Alan Stubbs and his team, as a player with potential, and played a big role in pre-season matches. Extra sessions, in particular with Assistant Coach Andy Holden, are designed to ensure his progress continues.

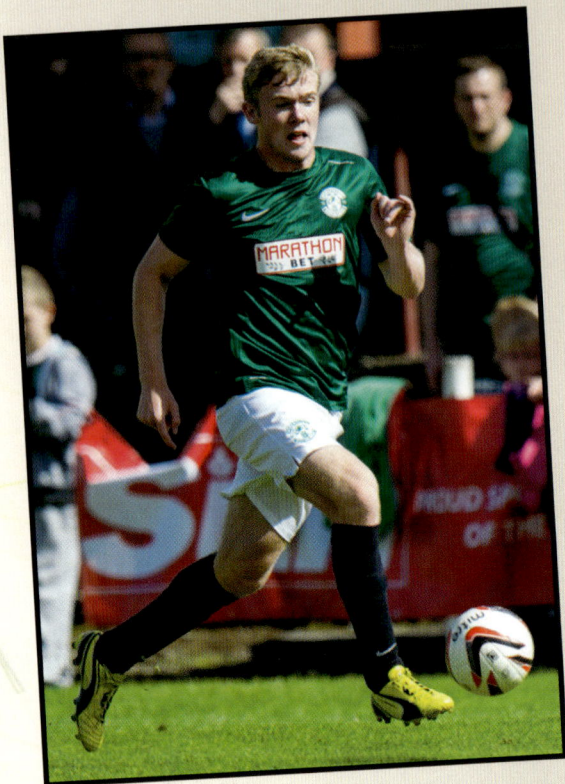

MAX TODD

•••••••••••••

Midfielder MAX TODD was another who played several pre-season matches and forced his way into first team contention.

Born in Sydney when his father was working in Australia, the 18 year old has come through the Academy. His Hibernian connection runs deep – he is the grandson of Bobby Kinloch.

Max is eligible to play for Australia – but his ambition is to play for Scotland.

KEEPER OXLEY JOINS HIBS

Goalkeeper Mark Oxley joined the club on loan from Hull City during the summer transfer window.

Oxley, 24, enjoyed a loan spell with Oldham Athletic last season where he recorded 43 appearances before his move north to Hibernian.

The 6ft 3in keeper has earned international honours with England at under 18 and under 20 levels.

HIBS CAPTURE SCOTT ALLAN

Scott Allan's capture during the summer transfer window was greeted with enthusiasm by Hibernian supporters.

The young midfielder was heralded as an emerging talent during his spell at Dundee United, before a move south to West Bromwich Albion, which saw him go out on loan to Portsmouth and Birmingham City.

The 23 year old has been capped at under 21 level for Scotland. He joined the Club on a two-year contract.

TEAM TAGS

Below are the nicknames various Hibernian players were tagged with over the years.

Can you match the 'tag' with the teammate?

LE GOD	JOHN HUGHES
THE PRINCE OF WINGERS	KEITH WRIGHT
THUNDERBALL	GORDON SMITH
BROONALDO	JOHN BLACKELY
YOGI	FRANCK SUAZEE
SLOOP	SCOTT BROWN
THE QUIET MAN	ANDY GORAM
KEEF	IAN MURRAY
THE GOALIE	PAT STANTON
NID	EDDIE TURNBULL

Answers on page 59

WORDSEARCH

Find the words in the grid. Words can go horizontally, vertically and diagonally in all directions.

W	M	R	F	Y	T	I	N	U	M	M	O	C
S	K	D	N	P	L	K	B	B	L	R	Z	D
L	K	J	E	W	H	R	L	H	V	T	A	N
L	W	N	Q	R	V	T	I	Y	E	O	R	J
E	Y	Q	I	Y	B	B	T	V	R	N	E	N
G	K	D	H	L	E	Y	I	R	C	E	D	D
E	Z	N	Y	R	H	F	E	B	N	E	I	N
N	R	B	N	Z	S	T	Q	F	N	R	N	A
D	B	I	P	U	S	Q	I	Q	P	G	B	L
S	A	F	O	A	H	I	B	E	E	S	U	T
N	D	M	E	G	T	M	Z	C	L	R	R	O
N	A	V	Q	B	V	T	L	M	Y	Z	G	C
F	P	V	N	E	M	H	S	I	R	I	H	S

Community ✓

Derby ✓

Easter Road ✓

Edinburgh ✓

Famous Five ✓

Green ✓

Hibees ✓

Hibernian ✓

Irishmen ✓

Legends ✓

Leith links ✓

Scotland ✓

Answers on page 59

MEMORABLE QUOTES

There have been some memorable moments throughout Hibernian's long and distinguished history, and some memorable characters. Here we revisit just a few, using the words of some legends themselves:

TOMMY PRESTON –
(on beating Barcelona in Europe – he scored in both the home and away legs):

"We played really well, but they lost the head at Easter Road. But for us to get that result was unbelievable. They'd just knocked Real Madrid out of the European Cup. We couldn't complain at all."

SIR MATT BUSBY –
(in the foreword to 100 Years of Hibs – he had played for the Club during the War years).

"I spent some of the happiest days of my footballing life playing at Easter Road.

"It gave me the particular pleasure knowing I had the luck to play behind a boy who was to become a legend in Scottish football, Gordon Smith."

LAWRIE REILLY – (on signing for Willie McCartney and his beloved Hibs):

"Willie McCartney was like the ringmaster at a circus, he just oozed personality and confidence. It was great to sign for the Hibs. I got £20 for signing, but I'd have done it for nothing at all."

JOHN FRASER – (on Eddie Turnbull's return to Easter Road as Manager):

"We'd been wearing tracksuits with wee holes in them for training. The training gear wasn't up to much. That all changed – new tracksuits, new training gear, everything neatly laid out for us before training. It was a different place altogether. He's the best coach I ever worked with."

EDDIE TURNBULL – (to striker Alan Gordon – a qualified accountant):

"The problem with you, son, is all your brains are in your heid."

ERIC STEVENSON – (on playing against Hearts):

"I loved playing against the Hearts. If you're a Hibs supporter, that is your Cup final. Whether it's a league match or an East of Scotland Shield game. I remember a game we were 4-0 up after ten minutes. I felt a bit embarrassed, because I started to take the mickey. If we'd kept our foot on the gas we'd have annihilated them that day."

EDDIE TURNBULL:

"There's class; there's first class; and then there's Hibs class."

57

QUIZ ANSWERS

Page 13 FIND SUNSHINE''S FLAG

Page 20 CROSSWORD PUZZLE

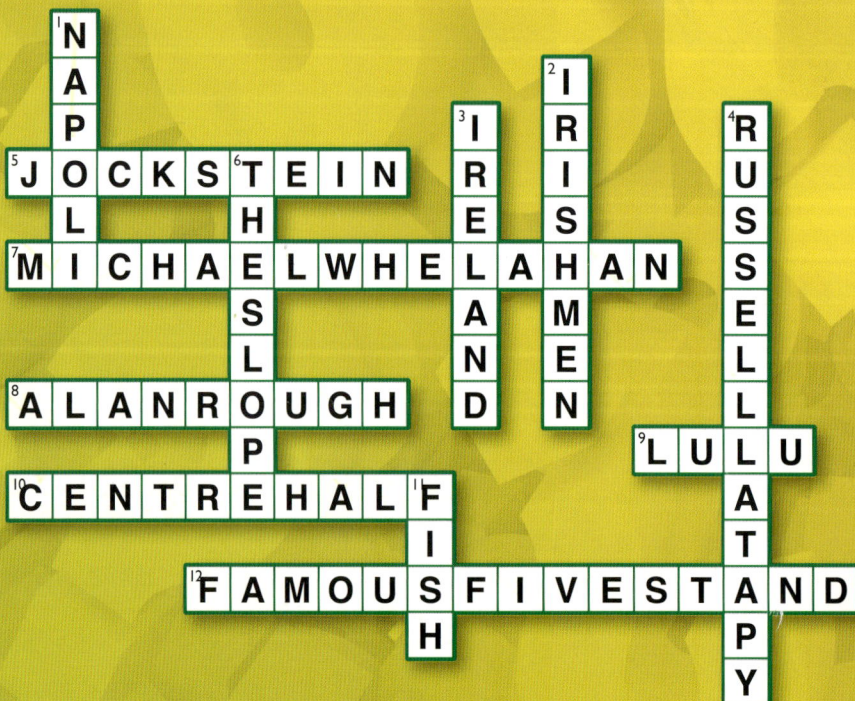

Page 21 FAMOUS FACES

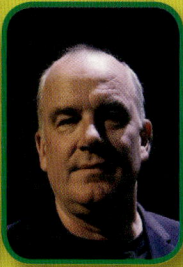

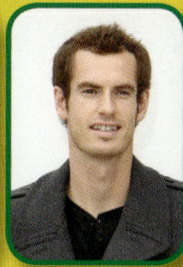

1. Gail Porter
2. Jack Docherty
3. Shirley Manson
4. Dougray Scott
5. Andy Murray
6. Irvine Welsh

Page 36 WHO AM I?

1. Franck Sauzee
2. Joe Baker
3. Lawrie Reilly
4. Gordon Smith
5. Pat Stanton
6. Arthur Duncan
7. Ian Murray
8. Andy Goram

Page 54 TEAM TAGS

Le God	Franck Suazee
The prince of Wingers	Gordon Smith
Thunderball	Eddie Turnbull
Broonaldo	Scott Brown
Yogi	John Hughes
Sloop	John Blackely
The Quiet Man	Pat Stanton
Keef	Keith Wright
The Goalie	Andy Goram
Nid	Ian Murray

Page 55 WORDSEARCH

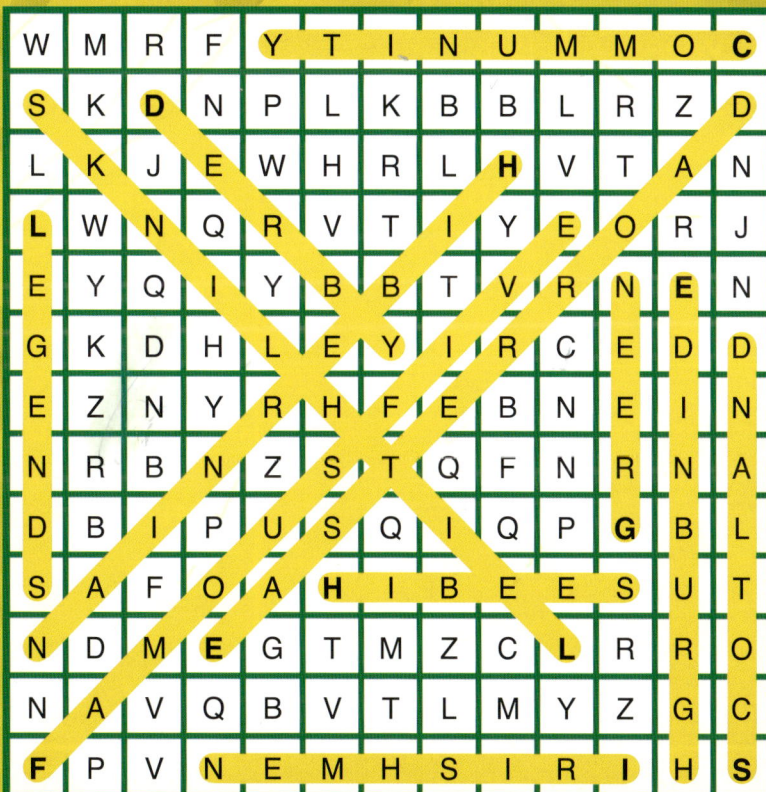

W	M	R	F	Y	T	I	N	U	M	M	O	C
S	K	D	N	P	L	K	B	B	L	R	Z	D
L	K	J	E	W	H	R	L	H	V	T	A	N
L	W	N	Q	R	V	T	I	Y	E	O	R	J
E	Y	Q	I	Y	B	B	T	V	R	N	E	N
G	K	D	H	L	E	Y	I	R	C	E	D	D
E	Z	N	Y	R	H	F	E	B	N	E	I	N
N	R	B	N	Z	S	T	Q	F	N	R	N	A
D	B	I	P	U	S	Q	I	Q	P	G	B	L
S	A	F	O	A	H	I	B	E	E	S	U	T
N	D	M	E	G	T	M	Z	C	L	R	R	O
N	A	V	Q	B	V	T	L	M	Y	Z	G	C
F	P	V	N	E	M	H	S	I	R	I	H	S

59

HIBERNIAN
HONOURS BOARD

SCOTTISH LEAGUE WINNERS

1902/03
1947/48
1950/51
1951/52

FIRST DIVISION WINNERS

1980/81
1998/99

DIVISION TWO WINNERS

1893/94
1894/95
1932/33

DIVISION ONE RUNNERS-UP

1896/97
1946/47
1949/50
1952/53
1973/74
1974/75

SCOTTISH CUP WINNERS

1887
1902

SCOTTISH CUP RUNNERS-UP

1896
1914
1923
1924
1947
1958
1972
1979
2001
2012
2013

SCOTTISH LEAGUE CUP WINNERS

1972/73
1991/92
2006/07

SCOTTISH LEAGUE CUP RUNNERS-UP

1950/51
1968/69
1974/75
1985/86
1993/94
2003/04

DRYBROUGH CUP WINNERS

1972/73
1973/74

SUMMER CUP WINNERS

1941
1964

CLUB CONTACTS

GENERAL ENQUIRIES

club@hibernianfc.co.uk

Tel: 0131 661 2159

MATCH DAY TICKETS

Book Online: Hibernianfc.co.uk

Email: tickets@hibernianfc.co.uk

Tel: 0844 844 1875

MATCH DAY HOSPITALITY

Tel: 0131 656 7073

MEETINGS & EVENTS

All Enquiries to:

Tel: 0131 656 7075

CLUBSTORE

hfcclubshop@justsports-group.com

Tel: 0131 656 7078